P9-BZT-704

WORLD'S
SCARIEST
PLACES

# HAUNTED
# BATTLEFIELDS

ALIX WOOD

Gareth Stevens
PUBLISHING

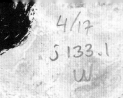

4/17
j 133.1
W

Please visit our website, **www.garethstevens.com**. For a free color catalog of all our high-quality books, call toll free 1-800-542-2595 or fax 1-877-542-2596.

Cataloging-in-Publication Data
Names: Wood, Alix.
Title: Haunted battlefields / Alix Wood.
Description: New York : Gareth Stevens, 2017. | Series: World's scariest places | Includes index.
Identifiers: ISBN 9781482459081 (pbk.) | ISBN 9781482459104 (library bound) | ISBN 9781482459098 (6 pack)
Subjects: LCSH: Haunted places--Juvenile literature. | Battlefields--Juvenile literature. | Ghosts-- Juvenile literature.
Classification: LCC BF1471 .W66 2017 | DDC 133.1'22--dc23

First Edition

Published in 2017 by
**Gareth Stevens Publishing**
111 East 14th Street, Suite 349
New York, NY 10003

Copyright © 2017 Gareth Stevens Publishing

Produced for Gareth Stevens by Alix Wood Books
Designed by Alix Wood
Editor: Eloise Macgregor

Photo credits: Cover, 1 © War Memorial Collection; 3, 10-11, 25, 27 © AdobeStock; 4-5, 24 © Imperial War Museum; 5 © Sonya Smith/ National Park Service; 6 © Miguel Vieira; 7 top & bottom © Alexander Gardner; 8 © Thomas Headley; 9 © R. Guthrie; 10, 11 © Deutsches Bundesarchiv; 12-13 © Sean Munson; 13 left © Donald Bain; 13 right © Shadowgate; 14 © Peter K. Burian; 15 © John Boyd Collection/Archives Publiques de l'Ontario; 16 Charles Henry; 18-19 © Martin Kelly; 18 © National Portrait Gallery; 19 © Tim Sheerman-Chase; 20 © Daniel Schwen; 21 © Angi English; 22 © Melvin Mason; 23 top © Gina; 23 bottom © Ron Zanoni; 24-25 © Danny Nicholson; 26-27 © Jörg Schultz; 28-29 © Vulkan-Avia; 29 © V. Menkov

Printed in China
CPSIA compliance information: Batch #CW17GS. For further information contact
Gareth Stevens, New York, New York at 1-800-542-2595.

# Contents

When a place has been the site of a terrible battle, it's not surprising it feels a little spooky.

A ghost is believed to be the spirit of a dead person. Ghosts are said to often haunt places where terrible things have happened. Battlefields certainly fit that description. Even if you don't believe in ghosts, most people agree that battlefields can have a very strange **atmosphere**.

Although the idea of ghosts is scary, these battlefield ghosts have never hurt anyone. It is as if they have come back to guard their territory once more.

The Stone House at Little Bighorn, Montana, was built as a house for the caretaker of the cemetery there. It is right in the center of the old battlefield.

The house has been the site of ghost sightings and strange events. Doorknobs have been seen turning by themselves. Lights are said to mysteriously come on, and loud footsteps and slamming doors have been heard.

One caretaker felt someone sitting at the foot of his bed. He said when he opened his eyes he saw the shadowy **torso** of a soldier with the head and legs missing.

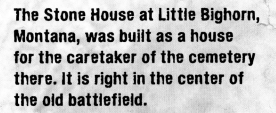

THE STONE HOUSE

# Antietam Creek, Maryland

The battle at Antietam Creek, in September 1862, was the bloodiest day of the American Civil War. A horrifying 22,717 men were killed, wounded, or missing. The sunken road known as Bloody Lane (below) is one of the spookiest areas of the battlefield. People have heard the sound of gunfire along the road and smelled smoke and gunpowder. Some have seen men dressed in **Confederate** uniforms walking down the path, and then suddenly vanish.

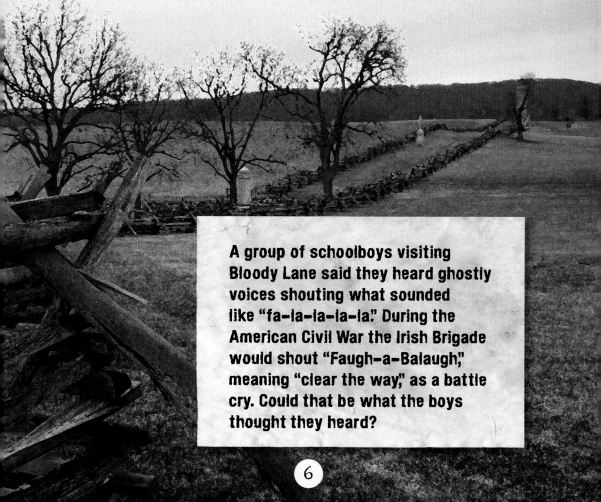

A group of schoolboys visiting Bloody Lane said they heard ghostly voices shouting what sounded like "fa-la-la-la-la." During the American Civil War the Irish Brigade would shout "Faugh-a-Balaugh," meaning "clear the way," as a battle cry. Could that be what the boys thought they heard?

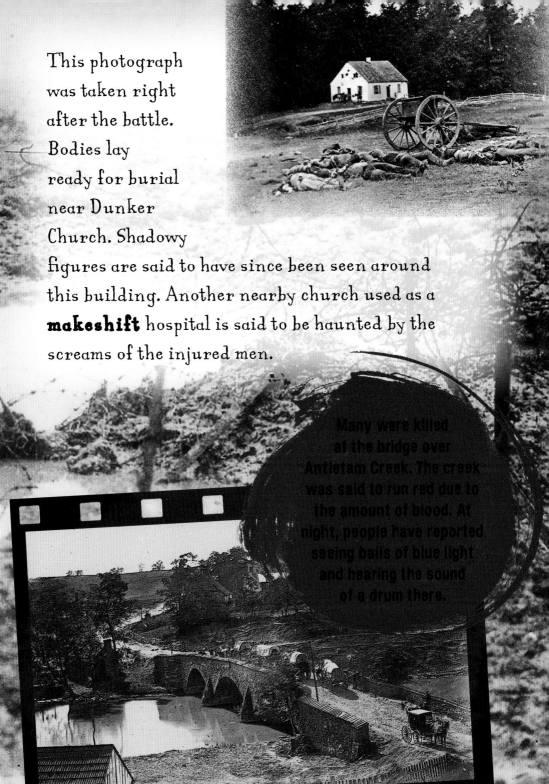

This photograph was taken right after the battle. Bodies lay ready for burial near Dunker Church. Shadowy figures are said to have since been seen around this building. Another nearby church used as a **makeshift** hospital is said to be haunted by the screams of the injured men.

Many were killed at the bridge over Antietam Creek. The creek was said to run red due to the amount of blood. At night, people have reported seeing balls of blue light and hearing the sound of a drum there.

# Marston Moor, England

One of the bloodiest battles during the English Civil War was at Marston Moor. Four thousand troops loyal to the King died on July 2, 1644. The battle took place during an evening thunderstorm. The Royalist troops were outnumbered and outsmarted. It was a great victory for Oliver Cromwell, leading the opposing side. It is said that some of the King's dead soldiers can be seen roaming the foggy moor.

THE OLD HALL WHERE CROMWELL STAYED BEFORE THE BATTLE

Local legend says that the ghost of Oliver Cromwell, dressed in armor, still haunts the village where he stayed on the night before the battle. He paces up and down, deep in thought.

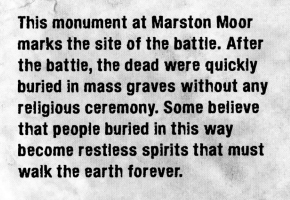

This monument at Marston Moor marks the site of the battle. After the battle, the dead were quickly buried in mass graves without any religious ceremony. Some believe that people buried in this way become restless spirits that must walk the earth forever.

The most haunted area of the battlefield is along a road that runs through the moor, past the monument. Several drivers have reported seeing people in what they at first believe are costumes, walking along or across the road. The figures suddenly disappear. There are no tall hedges or ditches at the side of the road where they could have quickly hidden.

# The Dieppe Raid, France

On August 19, 1942, an **Allied** attack was launched on the German-**occupied** port of Dieppe, France. Around 6,000 men, mainly Canadians, landed on the beach. The attack did not go well. Those planning the raid had to use vacation photographs to try to assess the slope of the beach. They got it wrong. Tragically, 3,367 Canadians were killed, wounded, or taken prisoner. The German army casualties were just 591.

Unknown to the Allies, the Germans had gun positions dug into the cliffs. As the troops landed on the beach, they were trapped. The Germans' machine guns mowed them down.

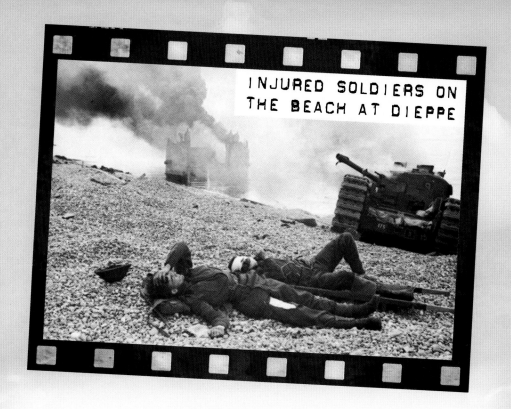

INJURED SOLDIERS ON THE BEACH AT DIEPPE

Nine years later, two English ladies on vacation in the area said they were woken by the sound of a battle. They heard machine gun fire, shouting, and explosions. There was a pause and then they could hear aircraft. They ran to the balcony overlooking the beach, but saw nothing.

Realizing that they were hearing something ghostly, they wrote down the times and the noises that they heard. The details of the battle were still top secret. Experts who studied their notes found the timings and the noises matched exactly with the order of events during the actual battle!

# Culloden Battlefield, Scotland

The Battle of Culloden, in 1745, was the **Jacobites**' final stand, and ended their attempt to restore a Stuart heir, Bonnie Prince Charlie, to the British throne. In around 40 minutes on that boggy, rain-soaked moor, around 2,000 Jacobites were killed. Only around 50 of the victors died.

Thirty wounded Jacobites took shelter in barns next to Leanach Cottage (above). The government forces found them. They barricaded the wounded inside the barns and then burned them to the ground. There is an **eerie** silence at Culloden. Near the Jacobites' burial mounds it is said there is never any birdsong, and no heather will ever grow there.

Ghostly soldiers are said to appear at Culloden on the anniversary of the battle. Loud cries and the clash of steel weapons have been heard. A tall, ghostly **Highlander** is said to wander the moor, whispering "defeated." In 1936, a woman lifted a tartan cloth covering one of the burial mounds and said she saw the ghostly body of a dead Highlander underneath it!

The chief of one of the Jacobite clans died next to this well. When a visitor once looked into the Well of the Dead, she saw the reflection of a Jacobite looking at her.

THE WELL OF THE DEAD

WELL OF THE DEAD HERE THE CHIEF OF THE MACGILLIVRAYS FELL

# Stoney Creek, Canada

In 1813, America attempted to invade Canada. The battle at Stoney Creek was ferocious. The British decided to make a night raid on the invading Americans' camp. With just 700 men against the 3,500 American troops, the raid was surprisingly successful and the Americans retreated. The British lost just 23 men, with 134 wounded and five missing. On the American side, 55 were killed or wounded, with around 100 reported missing.

These Stoney Creek battle reenactors are real. However, sometimes, ghostly soldiers are said to be seen marching across the field, as if to battle.

The home of widow Mary Gage and her two children lay right in the middle of the battlefield. During the battle at Stoney Creek, the house was taken by the invading American troops to be their headquarters. Mary and her children were held captive in the cellar.

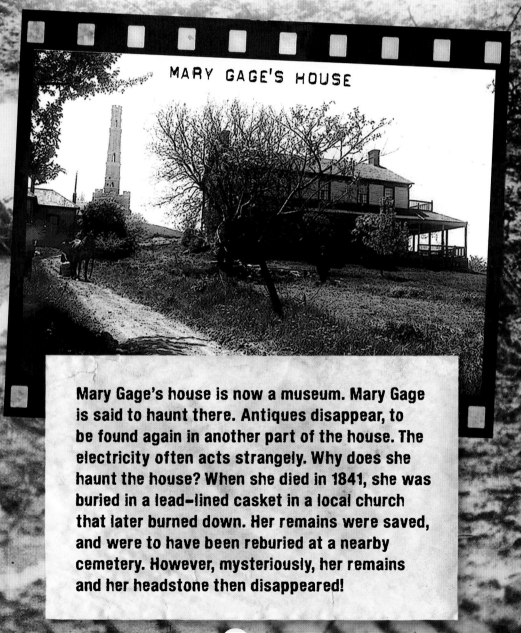

MARY GAGE'S HOUSE

Mary Gage's house is now a museum. Mary Gage is said to haunt there. Antiques disappear, to be found again in another part of the house. The electricity often acts strangely. Why does she haunt the house? When she died in 1841, she was buried in a lead-lined casket in a local church that later burned down. Her remains were saved, and were to have been reburied at a nearby cemetery. However, mysteriously, her remains and her headstone then disappeared!

# Fort Concho, Texas

Fort Concho was built to protect settlements in West Texas. It saw several battles during the years against the Comanche and illegal trading gangs. A row of officers' houses is the most haunted area of the site. Colonel Grierson's 12-year-old daughter Edith died in an upstairs bedroom. She was very fond of playing **jacks**. She now quietly haunts her old house.

Edith's ghost is often said to be seen at the house playing jacks on the floor of her room. People who say they have seen her say that the room suddenly seems very cold while she is present.

OFFICERS ROW

The headquarters building is also said to be haunted. One Christmas, a member of staff was tending the fireplace when a shadowy figure swept past him. After doing some research, the staff member found that a Sergeant Cunningham had died in the barracks after suffering from liver disease. He died on Christmas Day!

One of Fort Concho's commanders, Colonel Ranald Mackenzie, is said to haunt his old house in Officers Row. A member of the staff was once knocked by a blast of cold air and heard the sound of knuckles cracking. Mackenzie had a habit of cracking his knuckles, so the woman was convinced his ghost had returned to the house.

COLONEL MACKENZIE

People have also heard the ghostly voices of the fort's chaplain and an officer's wife. Staff have experienced lights flashing on and off, or heard heavy, ghostly boots walking on the porch!

17

# Edge Hill, England

Edge Hill was the first major battle of the English Civil War. The King's army was at war with Parliament, and both raised large armies. In October, 1642, the armies unexpectedly found they were near each other. Around 30,000 soldiers fought in a fierce battle that ended up a draw. The dead and dying were left where they lay.

Sir Edmund Verney (left) was the King's standard bearer. When captured, he refused to give up the flag to his enemy. They chopped off his hand, still holding the pole, and then killed him. His hand apparently continued gripping the pole for some time!

A BATTLE REENACTMENT

This was not to be the last time Verney fought in battle, though! Two months later, shepherds crossing the battlefield heard the terrifying sounds of war and, looking up, saw the battle taking place in the night sky. Other people say they saw similar events in the next months and a leaflet was written about the strange happenings.

The King sent men to investigate. They too saw the ghost battle and even identified Sir Edmund Verney and some of the other soldiers taking part! Screams, cannon fire and the thunder of hooves can still sometimes be heard to this day.

# The Alamo, Texas

Several ghosts have been seen at this old Catholic mission since the famous battle of the Alamo. Mexican General Santa Anna fought Texans guarding the fortified settlement. By the end of the battle, all the Texans and several hundred Mexican soldiers were dead.

Santa Anna sent men to burn what was left of the Alamo. His soldiers fled when they saw six ghosts appear at the mission's door, waving flaming swords and shouting "Do not touch the Alamo!"

THE ALAMO MISSION

THE OLD BARRACKS

Other ghosts said to roam the walls include Davy Crockett, who died during the battle. He has been seen standing at attention, holding a rifle. Often in March, people hear the sound of horses' hooves on the pavement. The ghost is believed to be a courier trying to return with a message.

Built near the spot where the Texan dead were burned, legend has it, a bookstore experiences books flying off the shelves. A corner of the store stays very cold. The bodies of the Mexican soldiers were taken to a spot that is now a children's park, which is also believed to be haunted. The Alamo is even said to be haunted by the actor John Wayne who starred in a film about the battle!

# Gettysburg, Pennsylvania

Over 50,000 men were slaughtered, wounded, or missing after the Battle of Gettysburg. This Civil War battle was fought over several days in early July 1863. The area is said to be haunted by many ghost soldiers, as well as Jennie Wade, a young woman shot while baking in her kitchen.

Daniel Lady Farm's barn (above) is said to be haunted by the ghosts of many soldiers who died there. The farm was used as a field hospital by the Confederates. Soldiers' graffiti can still be seen on the barn walls. Crime scene experts have found bloodstains in the house and barn. The ghosts are said to cause the air to get warm, electronics to act oddly, and strange smells to occur!

In 1993, actors filming a show about Gettysburg were sitting on this hill at the battle site. An old soldier in a tattered uniform talked to them about the battle and gave them some antique bullets. The man vanished. The bullets were from the 1850s!

Some people have experienced a feeling as if someone is pushing them over while walking across the battlefield. The dead were left in shallow graves at the battlefield for seven years before given a proper burial. Perhaps this led to so many restless ghosts?

A STATUE AT GETTYSBURG OF A FALLEN SON

# Glencoe, Scotland

In 1691, the King made all Highland chiefs take an **oath of loyalty**. The chief of the MacIain MacDonalds of Glencoe was held up by bad weather and missed the deadline by two days. Forces were sent to make an example of his clan. Captain Robert Campbell and his men pretended to be visitors and enjoyed the MacDonalds' hospitality. Then, just before dawn on February 13, 1692, they set about murdering their hosts in their sleep!

Ghostly men playing **bagpipes** (left) are said to have haunted Campbell's men after the attack. The sound of the pipes is sometimes heard echoing around the valley.

In homes all along the valley, 38 unsuspecting Glencoe MacDonalds were killed. Campbell's men then set fire to their village. Some of the MacDonalds managed to escape to the freezing snow-covered hills. Many more died from cold.

Visitors to the valley have since seen ghostly figures taking shelter on the hillsides. Some have said they have even seen ghostly reenactments of the battle. This often happens on February 13, the anniversary of the massacre.

Since the massacre, the playing card the nine of diamonds has been known as the "Curse of Scotland." It is believed the order for the massacre was written on this card.

# The Battle of Cannae, Italy

On August 2, 216 BC, Hannibal led his African army into battle against a much larger Roman army. Hannibal won the battle, and his tactics have gone down in history as being truly cunning. He managed to encircle the large Roman army and wiped them all out. It is believed around 60,000 – 70,000 Romans were killed or captured!

THE BATTLE OF CANNAE

CANNAE MEMORIAL

The battle killed more Romans in a single day than the U.S. lost during the entire Vietnam War. The battlefield is said to be haunted by their spirits. There is a legend that if you happen to see a ghostly Roman soldier waving a sword, you must not let him see you. If he does, you will be beheaded before midnight!

For hundreds of years since the battle, people have spoken of seeing ghost soldiers returning to the battle site. The soldiers are believed to have come back to protect Italy.

# Makaryev Monastery, Russia

According to the legend, The Makaryev Monastery was **founded** by Saint Macarius in the early 1400s. In 1439, the monastery was burned down by invading **Tatar** Khan Olug Moxammat, and most of the monks were killed. Macarius was taken prisoner, but later released.

Some of the worst fighting during World War II took place in Russia. Over 20 million Russians died during the conflict. Many bodies were hurriedly buried in the area around Makaryev Monastery. War souvenirs became popular with collectors. People would look for soldiers' bodies in order to find and sell collectibles.

The local dead may not have liked having their graves disturbed! People say a strange, ghostly fire was once seen at the monastery by men robbing graves for goods to sell. The grave robbers saw what they thought was a bonfire. Then they noticed the fire was suspended in midair! As they got closer, the fire disappeared.

The same robbers slept near the monastery, and woke to hear one of their group screaming. He had wandered into the forest and had seen something so terrifying he could not even speak about it!

Some ghosts are good. After Saint Macarius' death, people were healed of disease after visiting his grave. His bones were moved when the monastery closed in 1929. In 1995, he was returned to Makaryev.

THE SAINT'S BONES RETURNING

# Glossary

**Allied** Relating to the forces united against Germany in World War I or World War II.

**atmosphere** The mood of a place.

**bagpipes** A musical instrument with an airbag and pipes that make sounds when air passes through them.

**clans** A group made up of households whose heads have a common ancestor.

**Confederate** A supporter of the Confederate States of America.

**eerie** Causing uneasiness.

**founded** Established.

**Highlander** An inhabitant of the Highlands of Scotland.

**jacks** Small six-pointed metal objects used in a game.

**Jacobites** Supporters of the deposed James II and his descendants in their claim to the British throne.

**makeshift** A temporary replacement.

**oath of loyalty** A promise to be loyal.

**occupied** Being forcibly controlled after a conquest.

**Tatar** A member of a Turkic people.

**torso** The human body except for the head, arms, and legs.

# Further Information

Rice, Earle, Jr. *Little Bighorn: History and Legend (Haunted Battlefields)* Kennett Square, PA: Purple Toad Pub Inc, 2015.

Summers, Alex. *Haunted Battlefields and Cemeteries (Yikes! It's Haunted)*. Vero Beach, FL: Rourke Publishing Group, 2016.

# Website

Ducksters information about battle sites of the American Civil War:

**www.ducksters.com/history/civil_war.php**

# Index

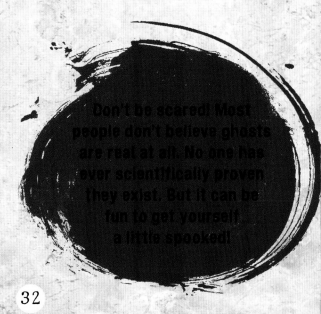

Don't be scared! Most people don't believe ghosts are real at all. No one has ever scientifically proven they exist. But it can be fun to get yourself a little spooked!